A Muse Her

Kyla Haynes

BookLeaf
Publishing

India | USA | UK

Presentation by *BookLeaf Publishing*

Web: www.bookleafpub.com

E-mail: info@bookleafpub.com

ISBN: 9789363304642

First edition 2024

To the younger me,

This collection of poetry is a testament to your courage, your resilience, and your unwavering spirit. You, who once felt trapped by the weight of unspoken thoughts and untold feelings, have found the strength to let your voice soar, your emotions flow, and your words dance upon the page.

As a woman who dares to embrace her vulnerability, her power, and her truth, you have unlocked a world of possibility within yourself. Through these verses, you have given voice to the silenced whispers of your past, allowing them to bloom into vibrant expressions of love, acceptance, and realization.

May these poems stand as a tribute to the journey you have walked, the battles you have fought, and the victories you have claimed. With each word penned, each emotion laid bare, you have shown the world—and yourself—the beauty of a soul unafraid to speak its truth.

So here's to you, to me, to us—may we always honor the voice within, the heart that beats with passion, and the mind that brims with creativity. Thank you for allowing the younger me to unfurl her wings and soar into the boundless skies of poetic possibility.

With love and gratitude,

Kyla

ACKNOWLEDGEMENT

I'd like to thank Book leaf publishing and to the man who inspired me to keep writing.

PREFACE

Attraction tangles down to my toes
Wrapping your arms around my conscience

Overbooked

Overbooked
"You look tired".
I am.
"Why?"

Insomnia

Awake at the thought of a sleepless mind
Curiosity roaming, ideas unaligned
Sleep the mind decline
Thinking of you is where I find
Restless conscience unspoken thoughts
Crowding the sleepless mind
Awake at the scenes replaying like an endless tape
Awake
I'm just....'
Wake

With you

Love is gentle
Love is patient
Love is kind
Love is sweet
Love is fun

Love is you!

The Mask

My smile does not define me
I said my smile, does not define me
You see there's more to a person than just a
smile. A smile can hide a million words mouth
sewn shut to fake the real shame.
Brokenness can smile while chained to sadness.
Why smile?
To keep from going insane, from committing to
darkness that overwhelms my vision
My smile does not define me
My smile is only an expression
Expressions we fake to hide our true demons
All it takes is a smile
I smile to mask my hurt from trauma
I smile because even when I'm down all I can do
is smile
Smile, you look pretty when you just….
Smile
Hiding from insecurities by just smiling causes
more hurt than not smiling at all
So why smile?
My smile does not define me
What does define me that you may ask?
My heart........

You may ask why do I smile?
I smile because I am hurt.

Again

Tired of playing games but constantly in love
with each other
Constant love, joy, and connections To the
constant bickering, attitude, and coldness
Attraction tangles down to my toes
Wrapping your arms around my conscience
that's gotten used to your bond you've seen since
the kick-off
Again we go with the cycle, which one of use
breaks?
Or someone has already broken

Seen

Have you ever been seen for you or seen
because of your actions?
Thoughts so loud
Mouth whispers nothing but silence
Seen to the point everyone notices but doesn't
see you
Seen where your presence is needed but always
never wanted?
Knowing the difference between seen for your
perception and seen for your imperfections
Have you ever been seen for you?

Grace

I saw her laughing at me, shaking her head in
disapproval
Taunting me with " it's not going to work".
Leaving her angel, procrastination, and his twin
self-sabotage
I saw her laughing at me like I was some toy
pulling my strings to get the crowd going
Joke after joke the laughter grows
I saw her laughing at all of my flaws and all Her
laughter is scarring
my mind is shackled by her beck and call
Why do she tourment me?
I am her joke,her punching bag to get a kick out
of
Seems like ending it would be a blast for her to
fully take over
Bonded by strings tight like a glove
Do you see her laughing?

.... I guess some jokes don't end

The mind

Healing is a journey of ups and downs twists and
turns
Journey to where?
Journey for me to wear and tear?
Outcome of many possibilities where you are
healed in the end
Happy, healthy and.... Free

Broken Promises

I'm sorry I left you, my mind wasn't right

Arriving Grey

Days are ending
Skies are gray
Dark clouds are forming crying red tears endless
of hurt and pain
Tomorrow is coming with the same cycle
When is it ever going to stop
Tearing down everything that was on top
Darkness clouded not light to see Backed in a
corner no room to sleep
Tiredness hooding my eyes making it hard to see
Hallucinating what should be
Dark days are forming
Into the clouded cloud smoke forming it's hard
to breathe
Scars piercing hidden from the world to see That
only the blind could see that the days are ending.

Scars

Scars?
Mental or physical?

.......both

Crazy of me

I almost lost my mind, thinking I wasn't good enough for you, I wasn't worthy of you, I wasn't right for you..... Or.. anyone I'm gladaaaad I realized who tf I was Who I am, and who is enough for me because a king who loves a black beautiful queen is worthy of each other, enough for each other, and is good for each other.
I'm glad I didn't lose my shit over you because I found my king!

Typical Delusion

I fell in love.....
With the love you portrayed
Silly me, it was your delusion Silly you, you fell
when I left...
Damn

X marks the spot

It's easy to forget something you've never had
People, lo.......
Easy to forget faces, places, and traumas?
The good traumas like family trips or making
bracelets with your best friend kind of trauma.
The good trauma.....
It's easy to forget the broken promises made
covered by small temporal conveniences
Conveniences made easy to promote the lack of
hope we promise to ourselves
Empty dreams of accountability that don't stay
true
It's easy to forget something you've never had
Longing for something to fill a void alcohol,
drugs, sex, people.....
I long for something... Something I want with
only him
A job only he can fulfill, I long for Forever.

Another application

Her skin color or her attitude that tricked your mind
Her words or her nappy hair that triggered your decline
Judging I see!
Reading a book without knowing its contents is ignorant
Nothing has changed, I see!
..... On to the next

Overtime

Tick tick goes the clock
Out of time the body goes to shock
Past memories replay the clock
Tick tock lifeline is on the chopping block
Tick tick... Tick tock
Body wavers over the grass
Tick tock its time to pass

Unanswered

All broken things seem to die slowly
Leaving things to heal time after time
Having nothing to mend
Slowly fading away as the darkness leaves
Bringing in a new fear for the mind to tend
Racing wonders leaving the mind to think
Anxiety building up borders around those walls
Walls so high the air is suffocating from that fear
in the mind
So broken that there is no wall to break down
So closed up it's hard to open up and tell
Scared that they might tell
Eyes roaming But mouth won't budge
Mind-wandering and wondering
Eyes leaking
Hands fidgeting
Holding it in to keep from saying what's wrong
What I feel is deeper than what I think I feel
Trying to find the right person to open up to
Now the darkness is gone the gray cloud appears
Waiting for the right moment to make its move
Leaving my pillow stained with tears
Tears that flow when I'm sad and upset
Upset that something isn't sitting right with my
heart
But what is my heart longing for?

Ms.Lover Girl

Sleepless nights
Restless days
Cold nights
Tired days thinking about you as the day plays
Mind wondering what could be
As my heart beats for what should be
Time and time I try to forget
As I remember the memories that won't forfeit
Day in and day out as time passed by
My heart tries to forget what my mind won't
comply
Sleep sleep the night away
Dreaming about the first day
Long gone your heart went away
That same heart I left astray
I love you is hard to say
Am I wrong to feel this way?

Those eyes

I keep getting lost in your eyes
Leaving you feels like suicide
Melting by your touch
Grazing my skin, my pearls clutch
Lost in your eyes
My soul feels like it's known you
My mind is trying to know you
My heart is digging you
Conscience asking why are you, you?
Lost in those damn eyes
Trying to find lies
Lies that lead to spies
Composing myself I improvise
Aching for more connection we share ties
Lost in those eyes, I see beyond
What you're trying to hide
Slick improvements I push aside
Emotions coursing through me
Desires longing to be free
I think I'm falling for those eyes

If whispers could sing pt 1

If whispers could sing I'd lose my mind
Already halfway there
Whispers are only just a whisper
Traveling as age grows whispers almost seem
normal, like a second thought
Silent dark space loud whispers only for you to
hear
She sang her loudest song
Whisper….whisper……whisper
Louder and louder I sunk into the deepest of
misery and she sung
Halfway there I could've sworn I'd lost it
My mind is halfway hers
Traveling and traveling with me as I travel
through this life, this soul, this mind
Whisper….
At it again a plague she is, a pain she was
She is bigger than war, the bigger she grows the
more minds she takes
Whisper….
Wavering, sucking life from its prey no matter
the day, her whisper

-Her deathly song

If whispers could sing pt 2

Silent sweet sounds of birds cover her melody
Swiftly the hymns of heaven dry her soft cries
A heaven she felt lifted from her shoulders
The light seeping through her thoughts
A light shed though she would never see
He was a breeze to her…. For her
Silently the whispers sing, smoothly sweeping
by the horrors away
Silently he slept through the night
Sweet soft silent
Silent the whispers sang